My First Book about the Alphabet of Mammals

Amazing Animal Books Children's Picture Books

By Molly Davidson

Mendon Cottage Books

JD-Biz Publishing

Download Free Books!
http://MendonCottageBooks.com

All Rights Reserved.

No part of this publication may be reproduced in any form or by any means, including scanning, photocopying, or otherwise without prior written permission from JD-Biz Corp and http://AmazingAnimalBooks.com.
Copyright © 2016

All Images Licensed by Fotolia, Pixabay, and 123RF

Read More Amazing Animal Books

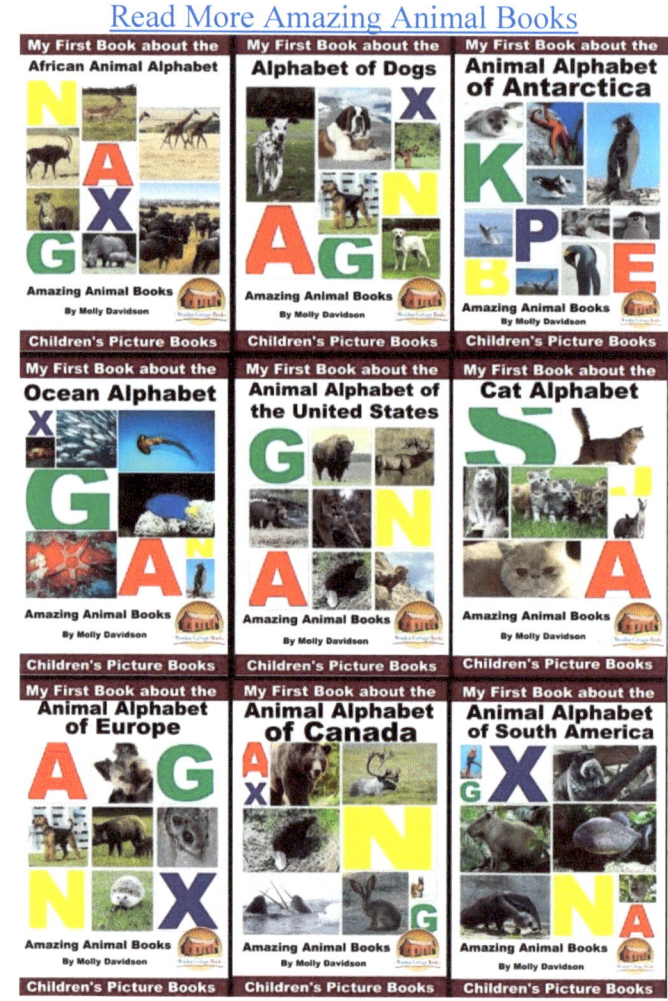

Purchase at Amazon.com

Download Free Books!
http://MendonCottageBooks.com

Introduction

Mammals are a type of animal which have hair or fur, give birth to live babies (do NOT lay eggs), and the babies eat their mother's milk.

A is for an Antelope.

Antelope live in Asia, Africa, and North and South America.

They usually have one baby, called a calf, after 8 months inside the mother.

Boys keep their antlers all year long.

 is for a Blue Whale.

Blue whales migrate to the colder Arctic and Antarctic Oceans in the summer and the warmer Atlantic and Pacific Oceans in the winter.

They give birth to a one baby, called a calf, after about a year developing in their mother.

C is for a Capybara.

Capybaras are a large rodent, which lives close to water in South America.

After 5 months, they give birth to between 1 - 8 babies, called pups, which can see, run, and swim within a few hours of birth.

 **is for a Dolphin.**

Dolphins like to swim in the warmer shallow waters around the coast.

They are pregnant for about 11 months, and then they have one baby, called a calf.

E is for an Elephant.

Elephants live in Asia and Africa.

They are the largest land animal, and they are pregnant the longest, 22 months!

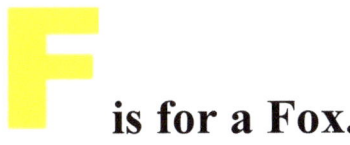 **is for a Fox.**

Fox hunt at night and live mostly in North America, Asia, and Europe.

It takes about 7 weeks for a mother to have about 5 babies, called pups, kits, or cubs.

They can run up to 29 mph (49 km/h).

 **is for a Giraffe.**

Giraffe live on the Saharan plains in Africa.

After waiting for 15 months, giraffes have one calf, which is already 6 1/2 feet (2 m) tall at birth.

They have black tongues which can be as long as 18 inches.

 **is for a Hedgehog.**

Hedgehogs have lived on the Earth for more than 15 million years in Asia, Africa, and Europe.

They will have 4 - 7 babies, which have no spikes, after about 40 days inside the mom.

I is for an Indri.

The indri is a lemur that lives in the rainforest on the island of Madagascar.

One baby is born in May or June after 5 months of developing.

Their yellow eyes help them measure distances between trees before they jump.

J is for a Javan Rhinoceros.

Javan rhinos are critically endangered and can only be found in the rainforests of south - east Asia.

It takes over a year for one calf to be born.

K is for a Koala.

Koalas live in and eat the Eucalyptus trees only found in Australia.

They give birth to one baby, called a joey, after about 35 days.

 **is for a Lion.**

Lions live on the open grasslands in Africa.

Mother lions will birth between 1 - 6 cubs after they have spent about 4 months inside her.

Lions can jump over 32 ft (10 m) to capture prey!

 **is for a Moose.**

Moose live in the colder northern forests of North America and Europe.

Mother moose will give birth to one calf, after about 8 months.

Boys will re-grow their huge antlers every year.

 is for a Numbat.

![A Numbat on the forest floor among dry leaves]

Numbats are marsupials that live in the forests of Australia.

They usually have 4 babies after only a few weeks of being pregnant.

O is for an Otter.

Otters live in oceans and freshwater rivers all over the World.

They give birth to about 3 babies, called pups, after 2 months.

They have thick, waterproof fur that helps keep them warm in the freezing water.

 **is for a Pademelon.**

A pademelon is a cousin of the kangaroo which lives in the jungles of Australia.

They give birth after 30 days to one baby joey.

 **is for a Quinling Panda.**

AilieHM © <u>Wikimedia Commons</u>

The Quinling Panda is a subspecies of the Giant Panda, which only lives in the Quinling Mountains in China.

After 4 - 5 months they give birth to two babies, but usually only one survives.

 is for a Rabbit.

Rabbits are found eating grass almost all over the World.

They are quick at having babies; it takes about a month for them to have 6 babies.

They are one of the top pets for children, because they are soft, kind, and small.

S is for a Skunk.

Most skunks live in North America.

Baby skunks, called kits, are born blind, toothless, and in groups of 6 after a few months of developing in their mother.

If they feel threatened they will spray a horrible smelling liquid from under their tail.

T is for a Thoroughbred Horse.

Thoroughbred horses are mostly used as a racing and jumping horse almost all over the World.

They carry their baby, called a foal, for 11 months before it is born.

 **is for a Uakari.**

Uakari monkeys live in the Amazon Rainforest in South America

They almost always give birth to twins.

 **is for a Vampire Bat.**

Vampire bats live in the tropical regions of Central and South America.

It takes between 3 - 4 months before the birth of one baby, which stays with its mother until it is about 5 months old.

 **is for a Warthog.**

The warthog is a subspecies of pig, which lives in the deserts of Africa.

After 5 - 6 months warthogs will give birth to 4 babies in their burrows dug in the ground.

Warthogs use their tusks to fight off predators, and the boys will use them to fight for the girls.

X is for a Xerus.

Xerus are a type of ground squirrel only found in Africa.

They are pregnant for 48 days, then birth one to three babies.

They live in groups, called bands, of up to 20 squirrels.

Y is for a Yak.

Yaks are found living in the colder mountains in Asia, where their thick fur keeps them warm down to - 40°F.

One calf is born in June, every other year.

Z is for a Zebra.

They live on the grasslands of Africa.

Mother zebras can have one baby, which is brown and white stripped, every year.

Their stripes help them blend in the tall grass, helping them stay hidden from predators.

Conclusion

There are between 4,500 - 5,000 different species of mammal.

All mammals are warm blooded, which means they make their own heat, they do not have to get it from the sun.

Download Free Books!

http://MendonCottageBooks.com

Purchase at Amazon.com
Website http://AmazingAnimalBooks.com

Horses
For Kids

Amazing Animal Books
For Young Readers
By John and
Annalee Davidson

Ponies
For Kids

Mendon Cottage Books

AmazingAnimalBooks
For Young Readers

Rachel Smith

Ten Amazing Horses For Kids

Nature Books for Kids
JD-Biz Publishing
K. Bennett

Akhal-Teke "The Golden Horse of the desert" For Kids

Nature Books for Kids
JD-Biz Publishing
K. Bennett

Suffolk-Punch "The Gentle Giant" For Kids

Nature Books for Kids
JD-Biz Publishing
K. Bennett

Shires "The great Horse" For Kids

Nature Books for Kids
JD-Biz Publishing
K. Bennett

Colonial Spanish "Horse of the Americas" For Kids

Nature Books for Kids
JD-Biz Publishing
K. Bennett

Canadian "The Little Iron Horse" For Kids

Nature Books for Kids
JD-Biz Publishing
K. Bennett

Cleveland Bays "History and Future" Horses For Kids

Nature Books for Kids
JD-Biz Publishing
K. Bennett

Our books are available at

1. Amazon.com

2. Barnes and Noble

3. Itunes

4. Kobo

5. Smashwords

6. Google Play Books

Download Free Books!
http://MendonCottageBooks.com

Publisher

JD-Biz Corp

P O Box 374

Mendon, Utah 84325

http://www.jd-biz.com/

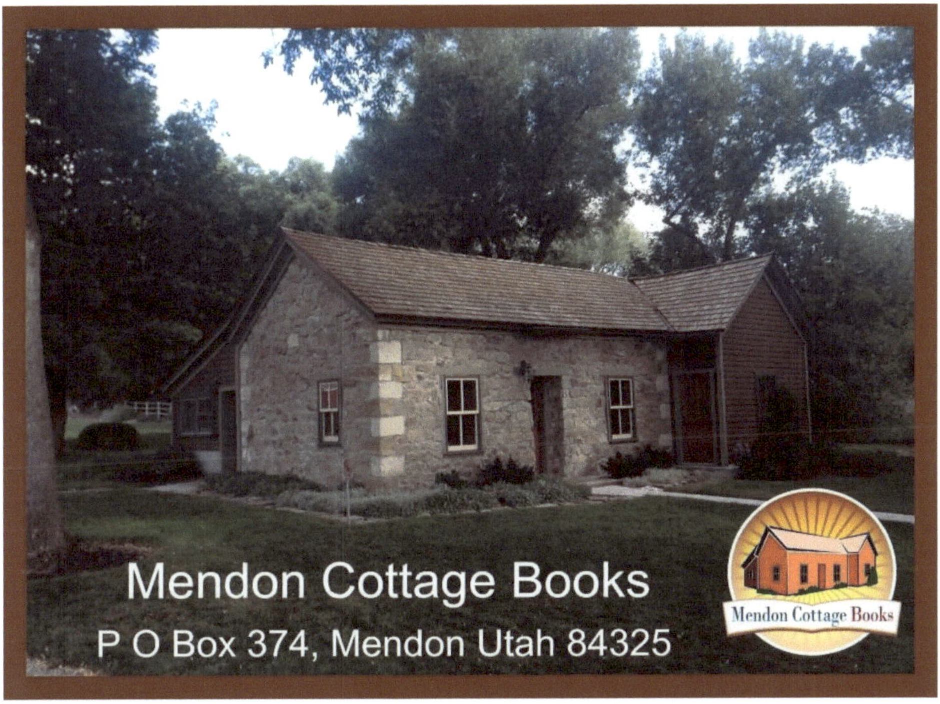

Mendon Cottage Books

P O Box 374, Mendon Utah 84325

www.ingramcontent.com/pod-product-compliance
Lightning Source LLC
Chambersburg PA
CBHW050902290526
45792CB00002B/673